LOS ANGELES

A **PHOTO**GRA**P**HIC **P**ORTRAIT

PHOTOGRAPHY BY STEPHEN BAY

Copyright © 2006 by
Twin Lights Publishers, Inc.

All rights reserved. No part of this book may be reproduced in any form without written permission of the copyright owners. All images in this book have been reproduced with the knowledge and prior consent of the artists concerned and no responsibility is accepted by producer, publisher, or printer for any infringement of copyright or otherwise, arising from the contents of this publication. Every effort has been made to ensure that credits accurately comply with information supplied.

Twin Lights Publishers, Inc. wishes to thank the organizations below for their permission to publish their trademarked images.

HOLLYWOOD™ & Design © 2006 Hollywood Chamber of Commerce. The Hollywood Sign™ and Hollywood Walk of Fame™ are trademarks and the intellectual property of the Hollywood Chamber of Commerce and licensed by Global Icons, LLC. All Rights Reserved. www.globalicons.com

The Jackie Chan™ trademark is used with permission from Mr. Jackie Chan.

Images of the Getty Center on pages 9, 10 and 11 are included courtesy of The J. Paul Getty Trust.

Images of the Walt Disney Concert Hall, the Dorothy Chandler Pavilion, and the Mark Taper Forum, are used with the permission of the Music Center of Los Angeles County.

First published in the United States of America by:

Twin Lights Publishers, Inc.
8 Hale Street
Rockport, Massachusetts 01966
Telephone: (978) 546-7398
http://www.twinlightspub.com

ISBN: 1-885435-69-X
ISBN: 978-1-885435-69-9

10 9 8 7 6 5 4 3 2 1

Editorial researched and written by:
Francesca Yates and Duncan Yates

Book design by
SYP Design & Production, Inc.
http://www.sypdesign.com

Printed in China

The City of Angels

From the moment it was settled by Spanish colonialists in 1781, Los Angeles' original name—*The Town of Our Lady Queen of the Angels*—foretold future greatness.

Unlike older, east coast cities, Los Angeles grew up just as automobiles were being mass-produced, creating an unprecedented urban sprawl and a network of freeways that today reaches into five counties and connects sixteen million southern California residents.

This urban sprawl has fashioned a distinctively bold and sassy metropolitan area where the scenery is always changing. Stephen Bay reflects the diverse character of this world-renowned city, from downtown's dramatic skyscrapers to distinctive neighborhood cultures. His images capture the allure of eclectic beach towns like Long Beach, Santa Monica, and Venice, ethnically rich districts like Koreatown and El Pueblo, the star-studded, magical attraction of Hollywood, and the glamour that is synonymous with Beverly Hills' mansions and shopping. Such is the famed depiction of the City of Angels, but she is also much more.

Los Angeles County alone is the site of over 40 institutions for higher education. Its internationally acclaimed private and public colleges and universities include UCLA, USC, Occidental College, Pepperdine University, Loyola Marymount University, California State University, Los Angeles, and California Institute of the Arts, to name only a few. It is no wonder that the area is also a hotbed of new technologies and research.

The Port of Los Angeles is the busiest in the United States with record volumes of cargo coming and going from the 7,500-acre harbor. With 43 miles of waterfront, the port offers a wide range of educational and recreational facilities. As a result, environmental management is critical, making the Los Angeles Harbor Department well known for its progressive environmental initiatives.

This sun-drenched city on the Pacific is a place where creative juices flow freely, whether expressed through innovative media technologies, breathtaking architectural design, or sidewalk graffiti and murals. It is the home of fine art at the Getty Center and the LA County Museum of Art, performing arts at UCLA and the state-of-the-art Music Center, as well as the sound stages of Paramount Pictures, Walt Disney Pictures, or Universal Studios where one person's idea transforms into the next blockbuster at your local Cineplex.

Theme Building, LAX

Built in 1961, this futuristic terminal resembles a landing spaceship. FAA Administrator Najeeb E. Halaby called it "the first terminal area specifically designed for the jet age." Hovering 70 feet above ground is the Encounter Restaurant, topped with an observation deck.

Pershing Square Park

Since its creation in 1886, design updates like a bandstand around 1900, the addition of fountains and palms in the 20's, and broadened paths in the 1940's have mirrored the city's cultural growth. The park was updated again in 1994 by architect Ricardo Legorreta.

Pershing Square Park

The stylish, five-acre public oasis reflects the modern views and colorful diversity of 21st century LA with its 120-foot purple tower, waterfall, and large orange spheres encircling a fountain. It also features a faux fault line that runs across the park. The wintertime ice skating rink is a favorite with all ages.

Runyon Canyon Park (opposite)

Comprised of 160 acres at the east end of the Santa Monica Mountains, Runyon Canyon Park rises to 1,320 feet at Indian Rock providing a 360-degree view that includes Hollywood, Wilshire Boulevard, and on a clear day, Catalina.

Getty Center Cactus Garden (above)

The Getty Center's dramatic landscaping is a sensory feast for visitors, with waterfalls, mazes, and scented foliage. The roof-top Cactus Garden at the South Promontory provides a perfect view of the valley's early-morning haze.

Entrance to the Getty Center *(opposite)*

Architect Richard Meier designed the complex to reflect both nature and culture. While inside, clear sight lines between the interior and exterior spaces allow visitors to move in and out of the five pavilions and always know their relative location.

Getty Center *(above)*

Amidst spectacular views of the Santa Monica Mountains, the Pacific Ocean and Los Angeles, the Getty Center is one of the area's most unique experiences. Its surroundings, inspiring architecture and depth of exhibits make the center a perennial destination.

Plaza Child Observer Preschool (top)

In Los Angeles, artistic expression seems to find its way to the façades of buildings and fences on every city block, whether it's a back alley in West Hollywood or this preschool for young Angelenos.

Downtown Los Angeles (bottom)

An international center of business and commerce, downtown Los Angeles is home to concert halls and a mecca for multicultural restaurants and shopping. Here you can find bargains on everything from electronics and clothing to jewelry and fine art treasures.

Walt Disney Concert Hall

The Walt Disney Concert Hall, part of the Music Center of Los Angeles County, opened in October of 2003. Architect Frank Gehry's striking stainless steel curves evoke the lines of a powerful masted ship with billowing sails. The interior's curved, sweeping lines are also a reflection of the building's connection to music. Gehry collaborated with acoustician Yasuhisa Toyota to ensure that this memorial to Walt Disney, complete with a 10,000-pipe organ, would be one of the finest concert halls in the world.

City of Gold

The setting sun casts a golden hue on the financial district as the rush-hour traffic finally quiets down. The center building is Wedbush Morgan Securities, headquarters for a major investment banking and financial services company.

The Beat of the City

Traffic is a red blur moving in and out of downtown Los Angeles. These skyscrapers in the heart of the city comprise L.A.'s financial district. The tallest downtown structure is the 73-story First Interstate World Center which, seen here at center, dwarfs its neighbors.

Los Angeles City Hall

Built in 1928, City Hall was the tallest structure in California until 1964 when building height limitations were lifted. The granite and terracotta façade was formed with sand from the state's fifty-eight counties and water from its twenty-one missions.

Bradbury Building *(top)*

Although its unassuming exterior is slightly Romanesque, this striking Victorian building is famous for its sky-lit, interior atrium, with dramatic wrought-iron railings and marble staircases, lift towers and glazed elevators.

Beloved Character *(bottom)*

In Los Angeles, you have a good chance of running into movie stars or, as in this case, statues of them. Silent-screen star Charlie Chaplin was the first international star of the modern era, especially beloved for his "Little Tramp" character.

Richard Riordan Central Library *(above and opposite)*

Originally constructed in 1926, this majestic landmark in downtown L.A. was influenced by the period's fascination with Egypt. The façade masterfully combines Byzantine, Egyptian, modern and Spanish themes. The central tower is topped with a tiled mosaic pyramid with suns on either side. At the apex, a hand holding a torch represents the "Light of Learning." Other design elements include mythical sphinxes, snakes and celestial mosaics. It is the third largest library in the country in volume of books and periodicals.

Westin Bonaventure Hotel and Suites (top)

Towering over a neighborhood rich in history, this downtown hotel enjoys a superstar status of its own and is one of the ten most photographed buildings in the world. Five, gleaming glass towers house 1,368 rooms and spacious meeting facilities.

Skyscrapers (bottom)

After oil was discovered in 1884, the City of Angels entered a new era. In the 1920's, while more oil wells hit pay dirt, L.A. became the state's largest city. By the 1970's, downtown developed into the largest banking center on the West Coast.

Wells Fargo Center (opposite)

Winner of many architectural awards, the 45-story KPMG Tower and its companion 54-story Wells Fargo Tower are joined by an elegant, three-story atrium that showcases one of Southern California's most significant sculpture collections.

Mark Taper Forum, Music Center *(opposite)*

The Tony Award-winning Center Theatre Group performs all year in the Mark Taper Forum and the Ahmanson Theatre at L.A.'s downtown Music Center. The Group is recognized as one of the nation's leading regional theatre companies.

Dorothy Chandler Pavilion, Music Center *(above)*

The Pavilion is home to the Los Angeles Opera and exciting newcomer, Dance at the Music Center. Under the leadership of famed tenor Placido Domingo, the opera company has become the fifth largest in the country.

Two Rodeo Drive *(top)*

When you think of the most exclusive and celebrated shopping in the world, Beverly Hills' Rodeo Drive comes to mind, and for good reason. The area is a top attraction for locals and tourists from all over the world.

L.A.'s Signature Sign *(bottom)*

Few street signs in America conjure up such a definitive image of glamour and mystique with wealthy celebrities furtively darting in and out of their favorite designer boutiques in hats and dark glasses, hoping to avoid the paparazzi and curious fans.

Beverly Hills Style *(opposite)*

Two Rodeo Drive is the lavish centerpiece of shopping with its Italianate architecture, fountains, and cobblestone walkways.

Beverly Hills Hotel *(opposite)*

The construction of this legendary "hotel of the stars" and home of the famous Polo Lounge in 1912, distinguished the new Beverly Hills residential community in L.A. from all the others in Southern California. The plan worked beyond everyone's wildest dreams.

Beverly Hills City Hall *(above)*

With its tiled dome, gilded cupola and eight-story tower, this elegant, Spanish Renaissance building has gracefully presided over Beverly Hills since 1932. Inside, terrazzo floors, marble walls and intricate ceilings add to its charm.

Will Rogers Memorial Park *(above and opposite)*

This beautiful state park was originally the private ranch of Will Rogers, the most beloved and highest paid actor in Hollywood in the 1930's. His spacious hilltop ranch in Pacific Palisades is located a few miles west of Beverly Hills.

A long winding road takes visitors up through dramatic California canyon country to reach the 186-acre estate, complete with corrals, horses, hiking and riding trails, polo fields, tennis courts, a ranch house and splendid, sweeping views.

Spanish Steps to Two Rodeo Drive (above)

Impressive stone and brass façades on both plaza levels at Two Rodeo Drive are connected by a shaded set of Spanish marble steps. The effect transports shoppers and visitors to the historic piazzas of the great fashion houses of Europe.

Beverly Hills Fountain (opposite)

Sweeping railings, marble fountains and urns bursting with floral color capture the romance and grandeur of old world elegance. No wonder this is a favorite spot for visitors to be photographed.

Walk of Fame *(opposite)*

Jackie Chan is one of more than 2,000 celebrities who are honored with a star on the Walk of Fame along Hollywood Boulevard. The Walk was created in 1958 by the Chamber of Commerce to honor special members of the entertainment business.

Hollywood Sign *(top)*

If it weren't for a fateful landslide, this famous 1923 sign might still read "Hollywoodland." Originally constructed to promote a real estate development, these big, blocky letters have become an internationally recognized symbol of fame.

Hollywood and Vine *(bottom)*

The intersection of Hollywood Boulevard and Vine Street became famous in the 1920's because so many radio and movie-related businesses were located there. Today the popular Hollywood Walk of Fame is centered on this intersection.

Goodbye, Norma Jean

Decades after her death, Marilyn Monroe's gravesite in L.A.'s Westwood Cemetery, is the most visited in Hollywood. Ex-husband Joe DiMaggio arranged her private funeral and, for many years thereafter, sent fresh flowers to her grave every week.

Hollywood Bus Top

A white, stretch limo tops this Hollywood bus stop shelter. Excessive and outrageous, the Hollywood community knows how to transform the most mundane, everyday experience into entertainment.

Capitol Records Building (opposite)

A landmark near the legendary intersection of Hollywood and Vine, the Capitol Records Building is the world's first circular office building. The 13-story tower resembles a stack of old 45's, and the sidewalk twinkles with the stars of Capitol's great recording artists.

Hollywood and Highland Center (above)

The lavish, multi-million dollar entertainment complex that defined downtown Hollywood's renaissance, the center includes the Kodak Theatre, home of the Academy Awards ceremonies.

Silver Gazebo *(above and opposite)*

On the west end of the star-studded Hollywood Walk of Fame, at La Brea Avenue, this sparkling silver gazebo features life-sized statues of four silver-screen goddesses in evening gowns. The gazebo's intricate spire rises twenty-two feet above the ground, embellished with the word, *Hollywood*. The statues are a nod to multiculturalism and honor the contributions of *(clockwise from top left)* Anna May Wong, Delores del Rio, Dorothy Dandridge, and Mae West.

Western Avenue, Koreatown *(above)*

South of Hollywood, Wilshire Center, also known as Koreatown, has been a strong community of ethnic culture and commerce. Recent upscale developments and a vibrant nightlife have also attracted Korean-Americans interested in a more urban lifestyle.

Ripley's Believe It or Not Museum *(opposite)*

Attracted to the bizarre? Ripley's museum will not disappoint you. Oddities such as a portrait of John Wayne created entirely from dryer lint and a statue of Marilyn Monroe sculpted in shredded money attract those with a curiosity for the unusual.

Charlie Chaplin Statue, Hollywood Entertainment Museum *(left)*

When comedic genius Charlie Chaplin made his entrance in silent movies in his too-small derby hat, too-large shoes and trademark moustache, he walked directly into the hearts of his audience and became a beloved global icon.

City of Angels *(right)*

Hollywood is a mecca for aspiring young actors and actors. Here, a friendly performer greets tourists outside of Grauman's Chinese Theater.

"You Are the Star" Mural

Painted in 1983, this delightful mural on Wilcox Avenue will stop you in your tracks when you notice famous movie stars in the audience. Muralist Thomas Suriya gave front-row seats to Marilyn Monroe, Lauren Bacall, Humphrey Bogart and Charlie Chaplin.

Directors Guild of America *(opposite)*

This signature steel-and-glass building on Sunset Boulevard houses a complex of three state-of-the-art theatres, an ideal setting for industry professionals to conduct private screenings of their films.

Norm's 76 Station, Sunset Boulevard *(above)*

The patriotic spirit is alive and well and living on Sunset Boulevard at Norm's 76 Gas Station. The American flag stretches across the entire length of the building.

Calling All Extras *(opposite)*

A surprisingly simple advertisement invites *real people* to apply for jobs as movie extras for a major motion picture with *lots of stars*. Perhaps the career of tomorrow's megastar begins here.

Sunset Boulevard *(above)*

In the early 1900's, motion picture production companies from New York and New Jersey began moving to California to take advantage of the reliable weather and longer days. The Nestor Company, Hollywood's first film studio, opened on Sunset in 1911.

Saddle Ranch

Take a quick trip to Texas when you come to this popular, country-western chophouse on Sunset Boulevard. With open-fire pits, fake horses, hay bales, live fiddle players and a mechanical bull, there's entertainment at every turn.

House of Blues

This legendary Sunset Strip club rocks seven days a week with hot performances by nationally and internationally acclaimed artists such as B.B. King, Isaac Hayes and The Pretenders. The House of Blues also features three friendly bars and a Southern-inspired restaurant.

Hollywood and Highland Station (opposite)

Original works from more than 250 artists make the Los Angeles subway stations some of the most unique in the world. At the Hollywood/Highland station Dworsky Associates architects created a dramatic design of lights, colors and curves.

Paramount Studios (above)

No two tours are ever the same at Paramount Pictures, as tourists visit the ever-changing sets of movies and TV shows. Paramount is the only major studio left in Hollywood where visitors have a unique opportunity to experience movie-making's colorful history.

Local Mural

In a back alley behind Melrose Avenue in Hollywood, an unknown artist had a vision that transformed an old wooden fence:
...and so we fix our eyes, not on what is seen but what is unseen, for what is seen is temporary...but what is unseen, ETERNAL.

Burst of Color

Since ancient times, people have felt the irrepressible urge to express their thoughts and emotions on public surfaces. Los Angeles boasts several thousand colorful murals and graffiti works by both well-known and anonymous artists.

Planet Ocean Mural, Long Beach Arena

When it was created in 1992, the monumental Planet Ocean mural on the exterior of the drum-shaped arena was the largest mural in the world, covering 116,000 square feet, and required 7,000 gallons of paint. Environmental artist Wyland depicts lifesize migratory, gray whales and other aquatic life found off of Long Beach. The multi-purpose arena is only one of the facilities at this complex that includes a convention center and the Terrace Theatre, a venue for local performing arts groups.

Queen Mary and Russian Submarine

The legendary, luxury-liner Queen Mary made her maiden voyage across the Atlantic in 1936. During her British commission as a World War II troopship she was nicknamed "The Grey Ghost". Available for tours, dining or overnight stays, visitors to this historic landmark may experience the elegant spirit of an earlier era. The Queen Mary's unlikely neighbor is a Scorpion Russian submarine, a previously top-secret Soviet Foxtrot class sub, was purchased privately from the Russian Navy in 1995, and since 1999 has been open for tours.

Long Beach Convention Center *(above)*

The Long Beach Convention Center is a world-class facility that hosts a myriad of events including commercial expos, colorful public festivals, and large-scale private functions.

Hyatt Hotel in Long Beach *(opposite)*

Sailboats bob in the calm waters adjacent to the luxurious Hyatt Regency Long Beach Hotel. Overlooking Long Beach Harbor, the hotel is adjacent to the variety of business and entertainment activities along the shoreline.

Watching the Action on Manhattan Beach

A telescope perched upon the 928-foot-long pier at the end of Manhattan Beach Boulevard offers excellent views of Palos Verdes and Catalina. Manhattan Beach is a hot spot for surfing, swimming and fishing.

Surfing at Manhattan Beach (top)

Just nineteen miles southwest of Los Angeles, on the southern end of Santa Monica Bay, you'll find a perennial favorite for all levels of surfers. Along with surfing are plenty of other thrill sports to enjoy on the water and in the skies above.

Manhattan Beach Police on ATVs (bottom)

Police patrol the busy beach, unnoticed by most sun worshipers. Others are fishing off the end of the scenic, 928-foot Manhattan Beach Pier or observing ocean life at the pier's Marine Studies Lab and Aquarium.

Union Station *(opposite and above)*

Across from historic Olvera Street, this landmark station deftly blends traditional Moorish and Spanish architecture with Art Deco. Renovated to its original splendor, the station is once again a busy transportation hub in downtown Los Angeles.

Built in 1939, Union Station was designed by the prolific father-and son-team, John and Donald Parkinson (see City Hall, page 16). Arched windows rise up to a lofty, fifty-foot ceiling, and outdoor waiting rooms feature beautifully tiled fountains and seats.

City of Dreams Mural by Richard Wyatt (above)

Magnificent Union Station is home to this dramatic 79 x 22-foot public-arts project. The mural depicts the rich, ethnic history of Los Angeles, from the original native Americans to settlers of the L.A. basin and contemporary Angelenos.

Union Station, Los Angeles (opposite)

Reminiscent of the glamorous era of train travel, this architectural treasure in downtown Los Angeles is one of the last of America's great train stations. The waiting room's terra-cotta tile floor features a central strip of inlaid marble in a stunning geometric pattern.

Los Angeles Memorial Colliseum

Adjacent to the USC campus, this beloved stadium has seen its share of heart-pounding games and roaring crowds as home to the Los Angeles Rams, the Oakland Raiders, USC's Trojans, UCLA's Bruins, and, briefly, the Los Angeles Dodgers.

Olympic Gateway

The familiar Olympic rings above the entrance to the Los Angeles Memorial Coliseum are a proud reminder of the Olympic track and field games that were held here in both 1932 and 1984.

Lockheed A-12 Blackbird

Lockheed-Martin is a leading developer of aircraft for the United States Department of Defense. This stealth weapon avoids surface-to-air missiles by merely accelerating. The Blackbird has never been shot down.

Lockheed F-104 Starfighter

The F-104 Starfighter was Lockheed's response to the U.S. Air Force's search for a smaller and simpler supersonic fighter after the Korean Conflict. Phased out of use by the USAF in 1967, the F-104 was known for its superb speed and acceleration.

Page Museum, Rancho La Brea Tar Pits

Five miles west of downtown Los Angeles, the Rancho La Brea tar Pits is one of the world's most famous locations for Ice-Age fossils. At the adjacent Page Museum, visitors can watch paleontologists clean, repair and store bones that are 10,000 to 40,000 years old.

Animal Statue, La Brea Tar Pits

Saber-toothed tigers, woolly mammoths and countless other prehistoric creatures that once roamed the area were trapped and mired in sticky pools of natural tar. Their misfortune has become a great boon for scientists studying the Ice Age.

Digging up Sloths, La Brea Tar Pits

Every year for a few months, natives and tourists can watch fossil diggers in action at this large, excavation site where an estimated three million Ice-Age creatures met their demise 28,000 years ago.

A Paleontologist's Dream Job

In one two-month period, paleontologists and volunteers collected over one-thousand Ice-Age specimens, including saber-toothed cat skulls, dire wolf skulls and the bones of giant sloths, horses, bison, coyotes, birds and rodents.

Royce Hall UCLA

One of UCLA's first buildings, magnificent Royce Hall was built in 1929 and modeled after San Ambrogio Church, a remarkable Middle Ages cathedral. Its unique Lombard Romanesque style prompted the State Historic Preservation Office to fully restore it.

Great Perfomances

Since its modest beginnings as a college auditorium, Royce Hall has matured into one of America's great concert halls where the sounds of song and dance's great masters still echo.

UCLA Library (above)

UCLA's renowned library holds a daunting ten million catalogued items within ten specific subject libraries. As one of the university's first four buildings, it is also an outstanding example of the Lombard Romanesque architectural style.

Kerckhoff Hall, UCLA (opposite)

UCLA's original student union was built in the lofty, Tudor Gothic style of architecture, and today houses the student government. With nearly 40,000 students, UCLA is the state's largest public university. L.A. is currently home to over 30 colleges and universities.

Los Angeles County Museum of Art

This world-renowned museum currently houses over 120,000 pieces in its permanent collection, including European, American, Islamic, Hindu, and Asian art among others. The facilities currently include six buildings on Wilshire Boulevard's "Miracle Mile" section, bordering the genteel Hancock Park neighborhood. Driven by its increasing collection and roles in the regional community, LACMA will be undergoing a transformation over the next five years with new galleries, buildings and façades.

Pavilion for Japanese Art

The Pavilion exclusively exhibits the extensive Japanese art collection of the Los Angeles County Museum of Art. Dating from 3000 B.C. to the twentieth century, works include Japanese paintings, textiles, sculpture, ceramics, and ancient artifacts.

Watts Towers Arts Center *(above and opposite)*

Without benefit of scaffolding, special equipment or drawing board designs, Italian immigrant Simon Rodia single-handedly built these unique and fanciful sculptural forms around his modest house in Los Angeles' Watts neighborhood during the period from 1921 to 1954. The tallest tower is nearly 100 feet high and contains the longest slender column of reinforced concrete in the world. In 1965, the Watts Towers Arts Center was founded to restore and preserve this innovative artwork.

McArthur Park

McArthur Park is an example of successful urban revitalization. In the early 1900's, it was a fashionable park with a man-made lake and paddle boats. By the 1980's, it was crime-ridden. Today this beautiful area is once again a safe and popular destination for families.

Promenade Reflection at Howard Hughes Center

The Promenade is an up-scale entertainment complex in this 70-acre business campus where Los Angelenos enjoy multiplex cinemas, IMAX, great shopping, fine dining, casual cafés, and a unique, glow-in-the-dark putt-putt course.

Randy's Donuts

Just a few miles north of LAX airport, Randy's is a sugar-fix destination with Hollywood star status. The 22-foot-diameter donut icon has starred in countless movies and TV shows over the years, while inside, the real donuts are delicious, as always.

El Capitan Theatre

The El Capitan Theatre opened in 1926 as a playhouse, and has recently been restored to its original splendor as a classic movie palace by the Walt Disney Company. In 1942, it hosted the world premiere of Citizen Kane. It now showcases Disney's animated classics.

Sculpture near the El Pueblo Historic Monument *(opposite)*

A big sombrero protects this whimsical musician from the noon-day sun on Olvera Street in El Pueblo, the birthplace of L.A. This Mexican neighborhood has dozens of landmark buildings situated around a traditional central plaza.

Biscailuz Building, Mexican Cultural Institute *(above)*

Originally the United Methodist Church Conference Headquarters in 1925, this building later housed the Mexican Consulate General. Today, visitors can view traditional and contemporary Mexican Art in the Institute's galleries.

Our Lady Queen of Angels Church *(above)*

Originally built in 1822 by the Franciscans, this is the oldest religious structure in Los Angeles. *The Annunciation,* a stunning mosaic mural by artist Isabel Piczek adorns an exterior wall.

Bell of Dolores, El Pueblo *(opposite)*

A gift from the Mexican government, the bell is a replica of Mexico's historic *Bell of Dolores,* rung in 1810 by priest Father Hidalgo summoning patriots to fight for their independence from Spain. It also signaled the beginning of democracy in California.

Olvera Street, El Pueblo

Located in the oldest part of downtown Los Angeles, Olvera Street is known as the birthplace of the City of Angels or "El Pueblo Historic Monument." Twenty-seven landmark buildings line Olvera Street, including Avila Adobe, the oldest house in the city (1818).

Colorful Mexican Culture *(left and right)*

Just one block long, Olvera Street is a popular tourist area that proudly displays the city's rich, Spanish heritage with traditional foods, music and colorful arts and crafts. Visitors can learn much about the history of the area by simply strolling the streets of this "Mexican village." This vibrant, historic area is a warm reminder of Los Angeles' humble beginnings as a simple, colonial Spanish village, settled by 44 pioneers in 1781.

Pagoda of Korean Friendship Bell

(above and opposite)

This pavilion shelters the massive Korean Friendship Bell at Angels Gate Park in San Pedro. It is carved and painted with intricate designs, and required ten months of careful assemblage by thirty Korean master craftsmen who were flown to San Pedro to construct the authentic pavilion. The pagoda is supported by twelve columns representing the twelve-year cycle of the Oriental zodiak.

Korean Friendship Bell, Angels Gate Park

This intricately-engraved, 17-ton bell and pagoda were donated to Los Angeles by the Republic of Korea in 1976 to celebrate America's bicentennial and honor Korean War veterans. The bell has no clapper, and is struck on the outside with a wooden log.

Angels Gate Park

Angels Gate is a stunning setting for the Korean Friendship Bell. Located at the eastern end of the rocky Palos Verde peninsula, the park offers panoramic views of Los Angeles harbor, Catalina Channel and the sea terraces of San Pedro.

Chinatown Doorway *(opposite)*

Today's vibrant Chinatown is actually L.A.'s second Chinatown and is the only Chinese community in America that was developed with a comprehensive community plan. The Union Station railroad station complex was built on the site of the first Chinatown.

Chinatown Parasols *(above)*

Chinatown is a unique and harmonious Chinese-American blend, the result of a collective community process. True to their architectural heritage, Chinatown buildings are distinctly Chinese with many cultural symbols inside and out.

Amusements in Chinatown (above)

Though much smaller than the Chinatowns of New York and San Francisco, great food, entertainment, and numerous small Chinese specialty stores abound in Chinatown's central Mandarin Plaza.

Chinatown Lanterns (opposite)

During its month-long New Year celebration in late January, Chinatown explodes with a mesmerizing display of sights and sounds including fireworks, the festive Golden Dragon Parade, a beauty pageant and a 5K/10K run.

Beads and Baubles

Half the fun of ambling along the streets of Chinatown is its eclectic collection of shops jammed with Chinese slippers, jewelry, trinkets, and china. Upscale stores specialize in Asian art, fine silks, inlaid furniture and other high-quality imports.

Hop Sing Tong Benevolent Association

At the turn of the 20th century, most of today's leading Chinese district associations, lodges and social clubs were founded. Church missions were also organized during this time. Thus began the process of community acculturation.

Grauman's Chinese Theater *(left)*

Grauman's grand opening in 1927 was the most spectacular theater opening in motion picture history. A riot broke out as thousands of fans tried to catch a glimpse of the glamorous movie stars and celebrities.

Arnold Schwarzenegger at Grauman's *(right)*

Match your foot and handprints with those of Arnold Schwarznegger and over 200 other Hollywood legends in this famous theater's courtyard. The first prints were those of the theater's co-owners, Sid Grauman and actors Douglas Fairbanks, Jr. and Mary Pickford.

A Majestic Landmark

Two massive columns support the bronze roof of Grauman's Chinese Theater which rises to ninety feet in height. Guarding the theater's entrance are the original, giant "Heaven Dogs" that showman Sid Grauman brought from China.

Yagura Tower (opposite)

The 60-foot blue-tiled Yagura (fire tower), which soars above the Little Tokyo skyline near the plaza, has already become a familiar landmark in Japantown.

Japantown (above)

Japantown is the social, cultural, religious and economic center of the largest concentration of Japanese Americans in North America. It had its beginnings in 1885 when an ex-seaman opened a restaurant on the west side of Los Angeles Street.

Venice Beach Art (opposite)

Venice was founded in 1905, mainly because its residents wanted to secede from Los Angeles. To this day, this beach town seems like its own universe. It is safe to say that Venice Beach will always be one of the most eclectic and effervescent areas of L.A.

Venice Canal (above)

Venice was constructed in 1904 as a replica of Venice, Italy—canals and all. A few of those original canals remain today, and they have been transformed into postcard perfection.

Graffiti Artist (above)

Vibrant, colorful art is still found along the walls of back alleys, but now many of these expressive murals also have a place in the Smithsonian's National Museum of American Art as well as other respected venues.

Gingerbread Court, Venice Beach (opposite)

Venice Beach has plenty of shops selling the kind of souvenirs you would typically expect to find at any popular beach area. However, this area also boasts upscale restaurants, high-end boutiques and galleries.

Venice Beach Boardwalk (opposite)

Venice hosts the world-famous annual Venice Art Walk. Thousands of people flock to Venice to walk through the studios and homes of the artists. Here, you can really get a feel for the creativity that abounds in this rare community.

Sand Sculptures on Venice Beach (above)

On Venice Beach, you can catch a few rays, watch a guy juggle three chainsaws or meet sand artists who create intricate and ornate sand sculptures like this fanciful flying dragon.

Venice Beach Patrol (opposite)

Police regularly patrol the busy sands of Venice Beach on horseback, as stars and celebrities brush up against the most eccentric beachniks.

Surfin' Safari (above)

As if summoned by a popular Beach Boys tune from the 60's, surfers challenge the waves of Venice Beach. Long recognized as a center for beach culture, the rolling surf at Venice has been a long-time favorite with locals.

Santa Monica Beach

A short drive from Los Angeles, Santa Monica Beach is a scenic getaway with sweeping coastal views. It blends seaside charm with the sophistication of an urban center at the edge of the sand.

Arlington West Memorial, Palisades Park

Located in a spectacular setting that overlooks Santa Monica State Beach and nearby Malibu, the Arlington West Memorial honors American veterans. Sandy walking paths lead to shady arbors and benches amongst the palms and fragrant eucalyptus trees.

3rd Street Promenade, Santa Monica

West Side Santa Monica's Promenade buzzes with celebrities and extraordinarily eccentric characters, day and night. This prime shopping, dining, and entertainment strip stretches for three excitement-filled blocks between the Santa Monica Mall and Wilshire Boulevard.

Santa Monica Beach at Sunset

In this idyllic setting between Malibu on the north and Venice Beach on the south, a couple walks barefoot on the water's edge in the midst of a spectacular Santa Monica sunset. The nostalgic Santa Monica Pier is silhouetted against the setting sun.

Musicians, 3rd Street Promenade *(top)*

Santa Monica street musicians entertain the bustling crowds on the Promenade. Off the street, many enjoy performances at numerous movie theaters, including a live magic show at the Magicopolis Club.

Santa Monica Beach Houses *(bottom)*

Beach bungalows and condos clustered all along this sparkling waterfront offer rental choices for vacationers eager to experience the California beach lifestyle. Grab a bike or rollerblades and ride for miles along a bike path in the sand.

Dinosaurs at the Gate *(opposite)*

Friendly dinosaur statues at the entrance to the 3rd Street Promenade greet visitors and delight children. Adults may have more interest in shopping or sampling the world-class cuisines of restaurants where even the chefs have earned celebrity status.

Street Performer on 3rd Street *(opposite)*

A brightly-clad street performer adds color to a Santa Monica sidewalk. The lively creativity of each act is part of the energy that flows from this seaside community.

Santa Monica Beach *(above)*

Home to snack shacks, seafood restaurants and a famous pier, Santa Monica Beach is a kaleidoscope of fun. On summer nights, the air fills with the hypnotic sounds of big bands, Miami-style Latin beats and everything in between.

Fanciful Seaside Placard Post *(opposite)*

A stroll down the Santa Monica Pier is a walk back in time to the glamorous, seaside resort days of Southern California. While storms destroyed many other piers, the Santa Monica Pier lives on as one of the last great pleasure piers.

Pacific Park, Santa Monica Pier *(above)*

Millions come to enjoy the rides and midway games at this unique *playland on a pier* that includes a vintage carousel of hand-carved horses that is documented as a National Historic Landmark. It was featured in the Academy Award–winning movie, *The Sting*.

Artist on Santa Monica Pier *(above)*

A young boy stops to watch a street artist paint brightly-colored postcards. Artisans throughout Santa Monica are an inspiration to all, young and old.

Chiat Day Advertising Agency *(opposite)*

Just like the award-winning advertising it produces, Chiat Day's headquarters in Venice stirs the imagination with cutting-edge design. Inside, innovative office design has reportedly decreased employee turnover by an incredible thirty percent.

101 Freeway from Mulholland Drive *(opposite)*

Freeway 101 is the most historic highway in California and one of the first U.S. highways ever commissioned. It runs from southern San Diego to Washington State. The downtown L.A. skyline is visible in the distance through an afternoon haze.

Pacific Design Center, West Hollywood *(above)*

With over 150 showrooms, the Pacific Design Center is the West Coast's largest facility for interior design products. It features the finest furnishings from all over the world, catering to interior designers and their clients.

Fireworks over Hollywood Bowl *(above)*

Summer home to the Los Angeles Philharmonic, the Hollywood Bowl is one of the largest natural amphitheatres in the world, seating just under 18,000 people. Often, during the summer, lavish fireworks shows rip through the sky, accompanied by live music.

Hollywood Bowl from Mulholland Drive *(opposite)*

In spite of wars, the Great Depression and social change, the Hollywood Bowl's seasonal music festivals have continued, becoming as much a part of Southern California's summers as beaches, movie stars, the Dodgers and Disneyland.

photo by Geronimo Quitoriano.

Stephen Bay

Stephen Bay is a California-based photographer, whose work has appeared in newspapers and magazines including the *San Francisco Chronicle*, *Gardening How-To*, and *Somerset Studio*. As a former Los Angeles resident, Stephen relished the opportunity to photograph and showcase his favorite city.

He was born and raised in Toronto, Canada and is the youngest son of Korean immigrants. He earned a degree in engineering from the University of Waterloo, followed by a Ph.D. in Computer Science from the University of California, Irvine. Stephen became interested in photography during his final year of doctoral studies and soon began offering his work to the public.

Stephen now resides in San Jose with his wife Kara, his dog and three pet rats. More of his photographs can be viewed on his website, bayimages.net.